FRIENDS OF ACPL

P9-CND-494

Thanksgiving

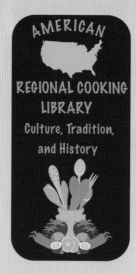

AMERICAN

REGIONAL COOKING
LIBRARY
Culture, Tradition,
and History

African American

American Indian

Amish and Mennonite

California

Hawaii

Louisiana

Mexican American

Mid-Atlantic

Midwest

Northwest

New England

Southern

Southern Appalachian

Texas

Thanksgiving

Thanksgiving

Mason Crest Publishers

Philadelphia

Mason Crest Publishers Inc.
370 Reed Road
Broomall, Pennsylvania 19008
(866) MCP-BOOK (toll free)
www.masoncrest.com

First printing
1 2 3 4 5 6 7 8 9 10

Library of Congress Cataloging-in-Publication Data

Sanna, Ellyn, 1958-
Thanksgiving / by Ellyn Sanna.
p. cm. — (American regional cooking: culture, history, and traditions)
Includes index.
ISBN 1-59084-624-9
1. Thanksgiving cookery. I. Title. II. Series.
TX739.S25 2005
641.5'68—dc22
                              2004005289

Recipes contributed by Patricia Therrien.
Produced by Harding House Publishing Services, Inc., Vestal, New York.
Interior design by Dianne Hodack.
Cover design by Michelle Bouch.
Printed and bound in the Hashemite Kingdom of Jordan.

Contents

Introduction
by the Culinary Institute of America

Cooking is a dynamic profession, one that presents some of the greatest challenges and offers some of the greatest rewards. Since 1946, the Culinary Institute of America has provided aspiring and seasoned food service professionals with the knowledge and skills needed to become leaders and innovators in this industry.

Here at the CIA, we teach our students the fundamental culinary techniques they need to build a sound foundation for their food service careers. There is always another level of perfection for them to achieve and another skill to master. Our rigorous curriculum provides them with a springboard to continued growth and success.

Food is far more than simply sustenance or the source of energy to fuel you and your family through life's daily regimen. It conjures memories throughout life, summoning up the smell, taste, and flavor of simpler times. Cooking is more than an art and a science; it provides family history. Food prepared with care epitomizes the love, devotion, and culinary delights that you offer to your friends and family.

A cuisine provides a way to express and establish customs—the way a food should taste and the flavors and aromas associated with that food. Cuisines are more than just a collection of ingredients, cooking utensils, and dishes from a geographic location; they are elements that are critical to establishing a culinary identity.

When you can accurately read a recipe, you can trace a variety of influences by observing which ingredients are selected and also by noting the technique that is used. If you research the historical origins of a recipe, you may find ingredients that traveled from East to West or from the New World to the Old. Traditional methods of cooking a dish may have changed with the times or to meet special challenges.

The history of cooking illustrates the significance of innovation and the trading or sharing of ingredients and tools between societies. Although the various cooking vessels over the years have changed, the basic cooking methods have remained the same. Through adaptation, a recipe created years ago in a remote corner of the world could today be recognized by many throughout the globe.

When observing the customs of different societies, it becomes apparent that food brings people together. It is the common thread that we share and that we value. Regardless of the occasion, food is present to celebrate and to comfort. Through food we can experience other cultures and lands, learning the significance of particular ingredients and cooking techniques.

As you begin your journey through the culinary arts, keep in mind the power that food and cuisine holds. When passed from generation to generation, family heritage and traditions remain strong. Become familiar with the dishes your family has enjoyed through the years and play a role in keeping them alive. Don't be afraid to embellish recipes along the way – creativity is what cooking is all about.

Thanksgiving Culture, History, and Traditions

The first winter was hard for the settlers at Plymouth. They were not used to such harsh winters, and they had barely enough food to get them through the long, cold months. Weakened and vulnerable to diseases, many of them died that first winter. The settlers must have wondered if they had been dangerously foolish to leave Europe and set off into the wilderness.

But those who survived the hard winter soon found that their new home had its own kind of plenty to offer. The Wampanoag Indians taught them how to plant and hunt, and by the following autumn, the settlers were enjoying a great bounty of food. They were so grateful for their change in fortune that their leaders decreed they would celebrate with their new friends by feasting and partying.

Edward Winslow, one of the early Pilgrims, wrote down this account of the first Thanksgiving:

> Our harvest being gotten in, our governor sent four men on fowling, that so we might after a special manner rejoice together after we had gathered the fruit of our labors. They four in one day killed as much fowl as, with a little help beside, served the company almost a week. At which time, amongst other recreations, we exercised our arms. Many of the Indians coming amongst us, and among the rest their greatest King Massasoit, with some ninety men, whom for three days we entertained and feasted, and they went out and killed five deer, which they brought to the plantation and bestowed on our governor, and upon the captain and the others.

William Bradford had this to add:

> They began now to gather in the small harvest they had, and to fit their houses and dwellings against winter, being all well-recovered in health and strength and had all things in good plenty. For as some were thus employed in affairs abroad, others were exercised in fishing, about cod and bass and other fish, of which they took good store, of which every family had their portion. All the summer there was no want; and now began to come in store of fowl, as winter approached. . . . And besides waterfowl there was a

great store of wild turkeys, of which they took many, besides venison, etc. . . . Which made many afterwards write so largely of their plenty here to their friends in England, which were not feigned but true reports.

After that first feast, however, the Pilgrims did not hold Thanksgiving again. Some of their descendents celebrated "Forefathers' Day," on December 21 or 22, as a way of remembering those who came before them. Several American presidents, including George Washington, called for one-time Thanksgiving events at various times of the year. The governor of each state often was the one to determine when (or if) Thanksgiving would be celebrated that year in that state.

Then in 1827, Mrs. Sarah Josepha Hale began lobbying for Thanksgiving as a national holiday. Finally, in 1863, President Abraham Lincoln set aside the last Thursday of every November as a time of national Thanksgiving; this date was near to November 21, when the *Mayflower* first anchored at Cape Cod in 1621.

More than seventy years later, President Franklin D. Roosevelt changed the date for Thanksgiving to the third Thursday of every November, in order to extend the Christmas shopping season, but in 1941, Congress permanently fixed Thanksgiving on the fourth Thursday of November. Meanwhile, in Canada, Thanksgiving is celebrated on the second Monday of October. The food traditions—turkey, pumpkin pie, cranberries—are much the same in both countries.

Today's Thanksgiving celebration is different from other holidays. It does not focus on any religious event or ritual; we do not give gifts; nor do we sing a set of specifically holiday songs or play particular holiday games. Instead, we simply join together around a table with family and friends. We remember all the ways we have been blessed, all the bounty that is ours—and like the Pilgrims, we celebrate our good fortune by eating . . . and eating . . . and eating. The food is the focus of the holiday. It is what we think of first when we hear the word "Thanksgiving."

Food is a powerful language. It communicates love and belonging; it expresses thankfulness and joy. This book will help you to prepare your own feast of gratitude, using the traditional foods and flavors of Thanksgiving.

Before you cook...

If you haven't done much cooking before, you may find recipe books a little confusing. Certain words and terms can seem unfamiliar. You may find the measurements difficult to understand. What appears to be an easy or familiar dish may contain ingredients you've never heard of before. You might not understand what utensil the recipe calls for you to use, or you might not be sure what the recipe is asking you to do.

Reading the pages in this section before you get started may help you understand the directions better so that your cooking goes more smoothly. You can also refer back to these pages whenever you run into questions.

Safety Tips

Cooking involves handling very hot and very sharp objects, so being careful is common sense. What's more, you want to be certain that anything you plan on putting in your mouth is safe to eat. If you follow these easy tips, you should find that cooking can be both fun and safe.

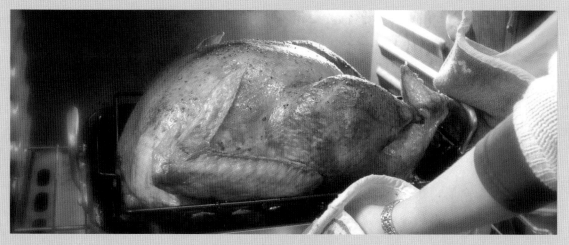

Before you cook...

- Always wash your hands before and after handling food. This is particularly important after you handle raw meats, poultry, and eggs, as bacteria called salmonella can live on these uncooked foods. You can't see or smell salmonella, but these germs can make you or anyone who swallows them very sick.
- Make a habit of using potholders or oven mitts whenever you handle pots and pans from the oven or microwave.
- Always set pots, pans, and knives with their handles away from counter edges. This way you won't risk catching your sleeves on them—and any younger children in the house won't be in danger of grabbing something hot or sharp.
- Don't leave perishable food sitting out of the refrigerator for more than an hour or two.
- Wash all raw fruits and vegetables to remove dirt and chemicals.
- Use a cutting board when chopping vegetables or fruit, and always cut away from yourself.
- Don't overheat grease or oil—but if grease or oil does catch fire, don't try to extinguish the flames with water. Instead, throw baking soda or salt on the fire to put it out. Turn all stove burners off.
- If you burn yourself, immediately put the burn under cold water, as this will prevent the burn from becoming more painful.
- Never put metal dishes or utensils in the microwave. Use only microwave-proof dishes.
- Wash cutting boards and knives thoroughly after cutting meat, fish or poultry — especially when raw and before using the same tools to prepare other foods such as vegetables and cheese. This will prevent the spread of bacteria such as salmonella.
- Keep your hands away from any moving parts of appliances, such as mixers.
- Unplug any appliance, such as a mixer, blender, or food processor before assembling for use or disassembling after use.

Metric Conversion Table

Most cooks in the United States use measuring containers based on an eight-ounce cup, a teaspoon, and a tablespoon. Meanwhile, cooks in Canada and Europe are more apt to use metric measurements. The recipes in this book use cups, teaspoons, and tablespoons—but you can convert these measurements to metric by using the table below.

Temperature
To convert Fahrenheit degrees to Celsius, subtract 32 and multiply by .56.

212°F = 100°C
(this is the boiling point of water)
250°F = 110°C
275°F = 135°C
300°F = 150°C
325°F = 160°C
350°F = 180°C
375°F = 190°C
400°F = 200°C

Liquid Measurements
1 teaspoon = 5 milliliters
1 tablespoon = 15 milliliters
1 fluid ounce = 30 milliliters
1 cup = 240 milliliters
1 pint = 480 milliliters
1 quart = 0.95 liters
1 gallon = 3.8 liters

Measurements of Mass or Weight
1 ounce = 28 grams
8 ounces = 227 grams
1 pound (16 ounces) = 0.45 kilograms
2.2 pounds = 1 kilogram

Measurements of Length
¼ inch = 0.6 centimeters
½ inch = 1.25 centimeters
1 inch = 2.5 centimeters

Pan Sizes

Baking pans are usually made in standard sizes. The pans used in the United States are roughly equivalent to the following metric pans:

9-inch cake pan = 23-centimeter pan
11x7-inch baking pan = 28x18-centimeter baking pan
13x9-inch baking pan = 32.5x23-centimeter baking pan
9x5-inch loaf pan = 23x13-centimeter loaf pan
2-quart casserole = 2-liter casserole

Useful Tools, Utensils, Dishes

baking sheet

casserole

cheese grater

chopper

cooking thermometer

slow cooker

electric mixer

flour sifter

food processor

muffin tin

paring knife

pastry cutter

potato masher

roasting pan

rolling pin

saucepan

skillet

Cooking Glossary

cheesecloth A very lightweight cotton gauze material.

cut Mix solid shortening or butter into flour, usually by using a pastry blender or two knives and making short, chopping strokes, until the mixture looks like small pellets.

fold Gently combine a lighter substance with a heavier batter by spooning the lighter mixture through the heavier one without using strong beating strokes.

food mill A kitchen utensil with a hand-turned blade that purees fruit and other foods, leaving the skin and seeds behind.

giblets The edible internal organs of fowl.

pinch An amount that equals less than 1/4 teaspoon.

puree A food that has been crushed into a smooth mixture.

simmering Gently boiling, so that the surface of the liquid just ripples gently.

spatulas Rubber or metal utensils used for scraping out bowls, spreading icings, or turning and lifting food.

stock A liquid in which meat, fish, or vegetables have been simmered; used as a base for gravy, soup, or sauce.

toss Turn food over quickly and lightly so that it is evenly covered with a liquid or powder.

tubers Short, fleshy underground stems, such as potatoes and sweet potatoes.

Special Thanksgiving Flavors

allspice

cinnamon

cloves

ginger

nutmeg

parsley

rosemary

sage

Thanksgiving Recipes

Roast Turkey

The center of almost every Thanksgiving dinner is the turkey!

Preheat oven to 325° Fahrenheit.

Ingredients:

one turkey, either fresh or frozen and defrosted
salt
vegetable oil
8–10 cups stuffing mix (if desired)

Directions:

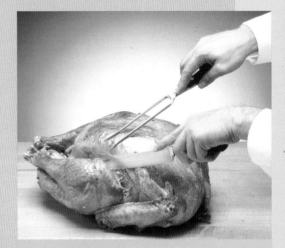

Cooking utensils you'll need:
roasting pan
wire rack that fits inside
the roasting pan
cooking thermometer
aluminum foil

Remove the package of **giblets** from the turkey's body or neck cavity. (The giblets can be used to make **stock** or gravy; see page 22). Rinse the turkey with cold water, inside and out; then drain and wipe dry with paper towels. Set the turkey breast side up (with the flatter side down) on a flat rack in the roasting pan. Rub the turkey inside and out with salt and then with vegetable oil.

If you're stuffing the turkey, now is the time to spoon the stuffing mixture into the neck and body cavities. Do not pack tightly, as it's important that the stuffing have a chance to cook thoroughly, so that all germs are killed. You don't need to fasten the openings shut.

You'll need to keep the turkey in the oven for 15 minutes for every pound that it weighs. In other words, a 16-pound turkey will need about 4 hours to cook. If you choose not to stuff it, however, 3 and a half hours should be enough.

After three hours of roasting, look at the turkey to see if the breast is golden brown. If it is, cover the breast loosely with aluminum foil so that it doesn't dry out while the dark meat continues to cook. If the breast is not yet golden brown, though, wait for another 15 to 20 minutes, and then check again.

About 30 minutes before the turkey is due to be done, insert a cooking thermometer into the thickest section of the thigh. Don't let the thermometer touch the bone. When the dark meat of the thigh is 180 degrees Fahrenheit, the turkey is done. The stuffing needs to be at least 160 degrees Fahrenheit at its center.

Using large spoons or *spatulas*, move the turkey from the roasting pan to a platter. Let the turkey sit for 20 to 30 minutes, and then carve the turkey by first removing the drum sticks, thighs, and wings, and then slicing the breast meat.

Tips:

If you don't want to bother with a cooking thermometer, many turkeys today are sold with a "button" that automatically pops out when the meat is the right temperature.

Prepackaged stuffing is easy to use—but if you don't have any on hand, you can make your own by chopping stale bread into small cubes (enough to make about 8 cups), adding a cup of diced onion, a cup of chopped celery, a cup of chopped parsley, salt and pepper, and a teaspoon or two of sage. Mix in 2 or 3 cups of chicken or turkey stock, and you're ready to stuff your bird.

Thanksgiving History

The Pilgrims and their friends the Wampanoag Indians ate wild turkey at their Thanksgiving feast. They also ate other wild fowl, like duck, goose, crane, swan, partridge—and even eagles!

Turkey Gravy

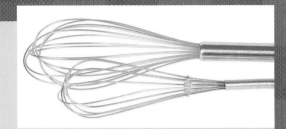

Ingredients:

drippings from the turkey's roasting pan
¼ cup white flour
warm stock or water

Cooking utensils you'll need:
measuring cups
medium-sized saucepan
metal whisk or wooden spoon

Directions:

Pour the drippings from the roasting pan into a large measuring cup. Skim off the fat. (It will rise to the top if you allow the drippings to sit for a minute or two without stirring.) Pour ¼ cup of fat into a medium saucepan. (You can discard the rest of the fat.) Stir the flour quickly into the fat.

Add enough stock or water to the remaining drippings in the measuring cup to equal 2 cups; add all at once to the flour mixture in the saucepan. Cook over medium heat, stirring constantly with a whisk or wooden spoon, until the gravy is thick and bubbly. Season to taste with salt and pepper. Makes 2 cups (about 8 to 10 servings).

Tip:

You can make turkey stock by *simmering* the turkey neck and giblets in several cups of water for a couple of hours. If you don't want to take the time, though, canned chicken broth will work instead.

Thanksgiving Tradition

Millions of Americans who arrived as immigrants between 1880 and 1921 learned about the history of their new country by celebrating Thanksgiving. The story of the Pilgrims now belonged to these newest Americans, who had their own reasons to be grateful for America's bounty. Thanksgiving's traditions became a means for uniting people from around the world into a single nation.

Today, we appreciate more than ever America's multicultural heritage. The United States is strong because of its citizens, people who come from around the world—Europe, Africa, the Mid-East, and Asia—as well as those who are native to this continent, the American Indians. The story of the European Pilgrims and the Wampanoag Indians sharing a harvest feast remains at the center of this very American holiday, challenging Americans today to unite as one.

Apple Stuffing

With more and more warnings about turkey safety, many cooks are choosing to pre-pare stuffing outside the turkey, to avoid the risk of germs infecting meat and stuff-ing that is not thoroughly heated. Stuffing is still served as a traditional accompa-niment to turkey—but it is often cooked on the stovetop or—as in the case of the recipe that follows—in a slow cooker.

Ingredients:

½ cup butter
1 cup chopped walnuts
2 chopped onions
one 14-ounce package of cubed
and seasoned stuffing mix
1 ½ cups applesauce
1 ½ cups water

Cooking utensils you'll need:
chopper
paring knife
measuring spoons
measuring cups
slow cooker
large skillet

Directions:

Melt 2 tablespoons of butter in a large skillet, add walnuts, and cook over medium heat, stirring often, until the walnuts are crispy. Remove nuts from skillet, place in a small dish, and set aside for later.

Melt the remaining 6 tablespoons of butter in the same skillet and add the onion. Cook for 3 or 4 minutes, stirring often, until the onion looks transpar-ent.

Lightly grease a 4-to-6-quart slow cooker with butter or oil. Put the stuff-ing mix in the slow cooker. Add cooked onion and butter, and stir gently. Then add applesauce and water, and stir lightly. Cover the slow cooker and

Apple Stuffing (continued)

cook on the low setting for 4 to 5 hours. Sprinkle with the toasted walnuts. Makes about 10 servings.

Tips:

When greasing pans, a healthy and easy alternative to butter or cooking oil is a no-stick cooking spray, sold in any grocery store.

You can use store-bought applesauce for this recipe—but it's also easy to make your own applesauce. Just cut a dozen or so apples into quarters, remove the cores, and place in a large cooking pot. (If you leave the skins on, you'll add color and flavor to the sauce.) Add ¾ cup of water and simmer for an hour and a half. When the skins begin to separate from the apple flesh, remove from heat and allow to cool for 15 minutes. Then pass the cooked apples through a *food mill*. Your arm may get tired, but the result is delicious! If you want, you can add sugar and a sprinkle of cinnamon. Then chill and serve.

Thanksgiving Heritage

Today's Plymouth has a Thanksgiving ceremony each year in remembrance of the first Thanksgiving. Wampanoag people still live in Massachusetts, and in 1970, one of them spoke at the ceremony to mark the 300th anniversary of the Pilgrim's arrival. Here is part of what he said:

> Today is a time of celebrating for you—a time of looking back to the first days of white people in America. But it is not a time of celebrating for me. It is with a heavy heart that I look back upon what happened to my people. When the Pilgrims arrived, we, the Wampanoags, welcomed them with open arms, little knowing that it was the beginning of the end. That before fifty years were to pass, the Wampanoag would no longer be a tribe. That we and other Indians living near the settlers would be killed by their guns or dead from diseases that we caught from them. Let us always remember, the Indian is and was just as human as the white people.
>
> Although our way of life is almost gone, we, the Wampanoags, still walk the lands of Massachusetts. What has happened cannot be changed. But today we work toward a better America, a more Indian America where people and nature once again are important.

Mashed Potatoes

Ingredients:

2 pounds potatoes, peeled and quartered
2 tablespoons butter
1 cup milk
salt and pepper to taste

Cooking utensils you'll need:
paring knife
measuring cups
electric mixer or potato masher
large cooking pot

Directions:

Bring a large pot of salted water to a boil. Add potatoes and cook until they can be split in half easily with a fork. Drain off the water. Put the pot back on the stove, over a low burner. Add butter and milk, and mash the potatoes (using either a masher or an electric mixer), until the potatoes are smooth. Add salt and butter to taste, and spoon mixture into serving bowl. Add a pat of butter to the top of the mound. Makes about 4 servings, so double or triple this recipe if you'll be serving a larger group.

Tip:

The paper wrapper on a stick of butter has measurements marked out on it, so that you can easily cut off 2 tablespoons of butter by following these markings.

Mashed Sweet Potatoes with Marshmallows

Preheat oven to 250° Fahrenheit.

Ingredients:

2 ¼ pounds sweet potatoes (either canned
or cooked ahead of time)
2 cups milk
3 tablespoons brown sugar
3 tablespoons melted butter
*a **pinch** of salt and pepper*
a dash of cinnamon
¼ cup raisins
a package of small marshmallows

Cooking utensils you'll need:
electric mixer or potato masher
measuring spoons
measuring cups
casserole

Directions:

Add milk gradually as you mash the sweet potatoes. Then mix in the remaining ingredients except marshmallows, and spread in a buttered casserole. Bake for 20 to 30 minutes, and then remove from oven. Cover top with marshmallows and return to oven until the marshmallows are golden brown.

Thanksgiving Food History

The Pilgrims and Wampanoags at the first Thanksgiving would not have eaten sweet potatoes—but sweet potatoes are nevertheless a uniquely American dish. They were first grown in Mexico, Central America, and South America, as well as the West Indies. Their botanical name, Ipomoca batata, was taken from the American Indians of Louisiana who were growing sweet potatoes in native gardens as early as 1540. The Indians referred to the sweet *tubers* as batatas.

In his first voyage to the West Indies, Columbus discovered many new foods, and sweet potatoes were among the treasures he brought back to Spain. The Spanish began growing them immediately, and soon they were exporting them to England.

In North America, Southerners from North Carolina, Georgia, and Louisiana adopted the name "yams" for the darker-skinned orange variety of sweet potatoes (although true yams grow only in Africa). Sweet potatoes soon became an important food on Southern menus. During the American Revolution and the Civil War, "yams" were said to have sustained Southern soldiers. Today, many Americans only eat sweet potatoes at Thanksgiving—but this all-American food is a nutritional powerhouse, rich in protein, fiber, vitamin C, and vitamin A.

Green Bean Casserole

Preheat oven to 350° Fahrenheit.

Ingredients:

two 15-ounce cans of cut green beans
¼ cup milk
one 10.75-ounce can of condensed
  cream of mushroom soup
one 2.8-ounce can of French fried onions
salt and pepper to taste

Cooking utensils you'll need:
casserole
measuring cup

Directions:

Mix green beans, milk, soup, and half the can of onions together in the casserole. Bake for 25 minutes, until bubbly. Sprinkle remaining onions over the top and return to the oven for another five minutes. Season with salt and pepper. Makes 6 servings, but this recipe is easy to double if you'll be serving a larger group.

Tip:

If you'd rather use fresh green beans, cut the tips and stems from the beans, and slice the beans into one-inch pieces. Boil in a little water or in a steamer for about 15 minutes (be careful not to let the pot boil dry), and then follow the recipe above.

Cranberry Dressing

Ingredients:

1 package raspberry or strawberry gelatin
1 cup boiling water
1 cup sugar
1 bag of fresh cranberries
1 peeled and seeded orange
1 apple, cored but with peel on
one 8-ounce can of crushed pineapple
1 cup chopped pecans or walnuts

Cooking utensils you'll need:
small saucepan
measuring cups
food processor

Directions:

Use a food processor to finely chop the cranberries, orange, apple, and nuts. In a saucepan, bring 1 cup water to a boil and then add the package of gelatin and the sugar. Stir until dissolved. Remove from heat and add fruit and nuts, including the juice from the pineapple. Pour into a serving bowl and chill until firm. Makes 6 to 8 servings.

Tips:

If you don't want to use fresh cranberries, you can use one 16-ounce can of whole cranberry sauce. You may also substitute 2 small cans of mandarin oranges for the fresh orange.

Thanksgiving History

In New England in 1670, John Josselyn wrote these words about cranberries:

> The Indians and English use them much, boiling them with Sugar for Sauce to eat with their Meat; and it is a delicate Sauce. . . . Some make Tarts with them.

Cheesy Scalloped Corn

Preheat oven to 350 degrees Fahrenheit.

Ingredients:

2 beaten eggs
two 16-ounce cans of cream-style corn
1 cup milk
1 cup cracker crumbs
½ cup chopped onions
½ cup chopped green peppers
1 cup shredded cheddar cheese
salt and pepper to taste

Cooking utensils you'll need:
measuring cups
cheese grater
mixing bowl
casserole

Directions:

Grate cheese. Beat eggs in a large mixing bowl. Stir in remaining ingredients, and spoon the mixture into a greased two-quart casserole (or you could use two one-quart casseroles). Bake uncovered for 35 to 40 minutes.

Thanksgiving Food History

Corn was an essential food for Native Americans, and they taught the first European settlers in Plymouth how to plant it and grow it. For the people of the Northeast, corn was one of the "Three Sisters"—corn, squash, and beans—the sustainers of life who protected and nourished the physical and spiritual well-being of human beings.

Roasted Winter Vegetables

Preheat oven to 450° Fahrenheit.

Ingredients:

2 potatoes
2 sweet potatoes
2 turnips
2 parsnips
4 carrots
2 stalks of celery

2 onions
3 tablespoons olive oil
salt
¼ cup fresh rosemary
2 tablespoons balsamic vinegar

Cooking utensils you'll need:
measuring spoons
measuring cups
paring knife
roasting pan

Directions:

Peel the potatoes, turnips, parsnips, and carrots. Cut all the vegetables into two-inch chunks. (The onions can be cut into quarters.) Put all the vegetables into a roasting pan and use your fingers to rub olive oil over them. Sprinkle with salt and half the rosemary. Cook in oven for 30 to 40 minutes, stirring the vegetables now and then, until the potatoes are tender when you poke them with a fork. Take the pan out of the oven, pour on the vinegar, and *toss* the vegetables. Sprinkle with the remaining rosemary. Makes 8 servings.

Tip:

4 tablespoons = ¼ cup. So if you measure out 2 tablespoons of rosemary, you will have half the total amount.

Don't worry if you don't have every one of these vegetables; it will still taste good, as long as you have the onions and celery to flavor the others.

Thanksgiving Food History

Corn was a very important crop for the Native people of the Northeast's woodlands. They ate corn at every meal, and it was their main food. They had many varieties of corn—white, blue, yellow, and red.

Cornbread and Cranberry Muffins

Preheat oven to 425° Fahrenheit.

Ingredients:

1 cup white flour
1 cup cornmeal
4 teaspoons baking powder
4 tablespoons sugar
½ teaspoon salt
½ teaspoon baking soda

1 cup buttermilk
3 large beaten eggs
¼ cup melted butter
or cooking oil
¾ cup whole fresh
cranberries

Cooking utensils you'll need:
measuring cups
mixing bowl
flour sifter
muffin tins
mixing spoon

Directions:

Sift together the flour, cornmeal, baking powder, salt, sugar, and baking soda. Make a shallow hole in the middle of the dry ingredients, and add the buttermilk and eggs. Stir just until blended, but don't stir too much. Gently stir in the melted butter or oil, and then *fold* in the cranberries. Pour batter into greased muffin tin. (Fill about ⅔ full.) Bake 15 to 20 minutes. Remove muffins from tins, and cool on a wire rack. Makes 1 dozen muffins.

Tips:

If you have a microwave, the easiest way to melt butter is to put it in a small microwave-proof bowl, and cook on high for about 30 seconds.

If you don't have buttermilk, you can add a teaspoon and a half of vinegar to a cup of regular milk to achieve the same chemical reaction that the buttermilk has with the baking soda. But don't try to make this recipe with regular milk and don't try to substitute baking powder for baking soda. Baking powder and baking soda are both "leavening agents"—that means they make batter rise when it's cooked—but baking soda requires an acid in order to work (such as that found in buttermilk, sour milk, or vinegar), while baking powder has the acid already included.

Pumpkin Crescent Rolls

Preheat oven to 375° Fahrenheit.

Ingredients:

*one 8-ounce package of cream cheese, softened (leave
at room temperature for at least a half an hour)
one 15-ounce can pumpkin
one 14-ounce can sweetened condensed milk
2 tablespoons flour
2 teaspoons cinnamon
1 teaspoon nutmeg
1 cup finely chopped pecans
four 8-ounce packages of refrigerated crescent rolls
½ cup sugar*

*Cooking utensils you'll need:
mixing bowl
electric mixer
measuring spoons
measuring cups
baking sheet*

Directions:

Use an electric mixer to blend cream cheese, pumpkin, condensed milk, flour, and spices until the mixture is smooth. Unroll crescent rolls, separate, and lay them flat on a baking sheet. Spread evenly over each uncooked roll one and a half tablespoons of the pumpkin mixture. Sprinkle a teaspoon of chopped nuts over the pumpkin mixture on each roll. Roll the dough into a crescent shape and sprinkle with granulated sugar. Bake 11 to 13 minutes until the rolls are golden brown.

Thanksgiving Food History

Pumpkin might have been one of the dishes at the first Thanksgiving—but it would have been cooked as a vegetable, rather than as a sweetened filling for breads and pies as it is used today.

Pumpkins and other gourds and squashes are associated in our minds with the fall harvest. For our ancestors, these were important winter foods, since their hard rinds meant they would keep through the winter, providing much needed vitamins and fiber during winter's cold, bleak months.

Piecrust

Pies of all sorts are the traditional dessert for Thanksgiving dinner. You can buy ready-made piecrusts—but making your own isn't that hard.

Ingredients:

2 cups sifted flour
1 teaspoon salt
⅔ cup solid shortening
2 tablespoons milk
2 tablespoons water

Directions:

Blend flour, salt, and shortening with a pastry blender; then add liquids and stir. Chill in the refrigerator for 15 minutes, so dough will not be so sticky. Use a rolling pin to roll out dough on a piece of waxed paper. When dough is about ¼ inch thick, center waxed paper over pie plate, with the pastry down, and peel waxed paper off the dough. Press dough evenly into pie plate and trim edges with a knife.

Cooking utensils you'll need:
flour sifter
measuring spoons
measuring cups
mixing bowl
pastry blender
rolling pin
pie plate
paring knife
waxed paper

Pumpkin Pie

Preheat oven to 400° Fahrenheit.

Cooking utensils you'll need:
electric mixer
mixing bowl
measuring cups
measuring spoons

Ingredients:

3 eggs	one 14-ounce can sweetened
¾ cup sugar	condensed milk
1 teaspoon cinnamon	⅔ cup half-and-half
½ teaspoon nutmeg	one 29-ounce can pumpkin **puree**
½ teaspoon ginger	1 piecrust for 9-inch pie
¼ teaspoon ground cloves	(either homemade or ready-made)

Directions:

Use the electric mixer to beat together eggs, sugar, spices, condensed milk, half-and-half, and pumpkin. Mix until all lumps are gone, but do not over-beat. Pour mixture into pie crust and bake for 45 minutes. Let cool and serve with whipped cream.

Tip:

You can make your own whipped cream by beating one cup of heavy cream with an electric mixer until the cream thickens. Add a teaspoon of vanilla and a half a cup of sugar and continue to beat until the cream stands in peaks. Don't keep beating after that, though—if you do, you'll end up with butter! And if this seems like too much work, the whipped cream that you squirt from a can is easier and almost as good.

Thanksgiving Food History

American Indians ate long strips of pumpkin roasted on open fires. The roots of pumpkin pie occurred when the European colonists sliced off the pumpkin top, removed the seeds, and filled the insides with milk, spices, and honey. The pumpkin was baked in hot ashes, and then eaten as a dessert.

By the eighteenth century, pumpkin pie had a top and bottom crust, and was filled with slices of pumpkin, alternating with layers of sugar and butter. By the beginning of the nineteenth century, pumpkin pie looked more like we think of it—with pureed pumpkin and a single crust.

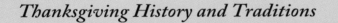

Thanksgiving History and Traditions

The feast that the Pilgrims enjoyed with their Indian friends was based on harvest traditions the Pilgrims had brought with them from England. These festivals were celebrated sometime around the 29th of September, after all the fruits, grains, and vegetables had been gathered in from the fields before the on-slaught of winter. These celebrations of plenty marked the end of months of hard labor; they were times of joy and triumph and feasting.

One of the important harvests for the early North American settlers was the apple harvest. Apples grew well in North America, and they lasted through the long winters, providing the settlers with fresh fruit for desserts. No wonder then that today we associate apples with autumn, with cozy meals at the end of cold days, and with Thanksgiving's bounty.

Apple Pie

Preheat oven to 425° Fahrenheit.

Ingredients:

⅓ to ⅔ cup sugar
¼ cup flour
½ teaspoon nutmeg
½ teaspoon cinnamon

pinch of salt
8 medium sized apples
2 tablespoons margarine
2 piecrusts

Cooking utensils you'll need:
paring knife
mixing bowl
measuring cups
measuring spoons
9-inch pie plate

Directions:

Peel, core, and slice the apples, trying to keep the slices about a ¼ inch thick. Mix sugar, flour, nutmeg, cinnamon, and salt in large mixing bowl, and then stir in apples. Spoon into pastry-lined pie plate, and dot with margarine or butter. Cover with top crust and seal the edges, either by pinching with your fingers or pressing a fork all around the edge. Cut slits in the top—if you want you can cut out flower shapes, make a face, or even cut out a short message. Bake 40 to 50 minutes or until crust is brown and juice begins to bubble through slits in crust.

Tips:

A medium apple = about 1 cup.

To keep edge of crust from burning, cover it with a 3-inch strip of aluminum foil. Remove foil during last 15 minutes of baking.

Apple Cranberry Cobbler

Preheat oven to 375° fahrenheit.

Ingredients:

5 cups peeled and sliced apples
1 ¼ cups sugar
1 cup fresh cranberries
3 tablespoons tapioca
½ teaspoon cinnamon
1 cup water
2 tablespoons butter or margarine
¾ cup white flour
2 tablespoons sugar
1 teaspoon baking powder
⅛ teaspoon salt
¼ cup butter or margarine
3 tablespoons milk

Cooking utensils you'll need:
large saucepan
mixing bowl
measuring cups
measuring spoons
2-quart baking dish

Directions:

Mix apples, sugar, cranberries, cinnamon, tapioca and water in a large saucepan. Cook over medium heat, stirring constantly, until mixture comes to a boil. Pour into a 2-quart baking dish, and dot with 2 tablespoons of butter.

Mix flour, sugar, baking powder, and salt in a large mixing bowl. Then *cut* in ¼ cup butter, until the mixture looks like coarse crumbs. Stir in milk to make a soft dough, and drop by tablespoons on the apple mixture. Bake 30 minutes, until topping is golden brown. Serve with ice cream or whipped cream (see page 48). Makes 8 servings.

Thanksgiving History

The concept of "thanksgiving" was a vital one to the Wampanoag. For many Native people of the Northeast, thanksgiving played an essential role in each of their festivals. This Thanksgiving speech was a part of every ceremony the Iroquois celebrated:

> This is what He-Fashioned-Our-Lives did: He decided, "The only thing required of those moving around the earth is that they express their gratitude." That is the obligation of those of us gathered here: that we continue to be grateful. . . . The first thing for us to do is to be thankful for each other. . . ."
>
> Then the Creator said, "The people will have love; they will simply be thankful. They will begin on the earth, giving thanks for all they see. They will carry it upward, ending where I dwell. . . ."

Thanksgiving History

Here are some other foods that may have been on the first Thanksgiving's menu:

- seafood—cod, eel, clams, and lobsters
- grain—wheat, Indian corn
- vegetables—pumpkin, peas, beans, onions, lettuce, radishes, carrots
- fruit—plums, grapes
- nuts—walnuts, chestnuts, acorns
- foods used as seasonings—leeks, liverwort, olive oil, dried currants, and parsnips, as well as spices such as cinnamon, ginger, nutmeg, and pepper

Pilgrim Table Manners

If you were a Pilgrim at the first Thanksgiving, you would have probably eaten from a wooden platter called a trencher. Each trencher had a dinner side and pie side, and it was proper manners to flip the whole thing over when you were ready for dessert. You would probably have used a napkin, knife, and spoon—but not a fork.

Believe it or not, you would have shared your trencher with the person next to you. If two unmarried people of the opposite sex shared a trencher, they were considered to be engaged.

Hot Apple Cider

This is a perfect beverage to go with a Thanksgiving meal.

Ingredients:

6 cups apple cider
2 cinnamon sticks
6 whole cloves
6 whole allspice berries
1 orange peel, cut into strips
1 lemon peel, cut into strips

Cooking utensils you'll need:
large saucepan
square of cheesecloth
string

Directions:

Pour the cider into a large saucepan and place over medium heat. Place the cinnamon, cloves, allspice berries, orange peel, and lemon peel in the center of a clean square of cheesecloth. Fold up the edges of the cloth and tie it with string. Drop the bundle in the cider and heat for 5 to 10 minutes, until the cider is steaming but not boiling. Remove the cider from the stove, discard spice bundle, and ladle cider into mugs, adding a fresh stick of cinnamon to each serving.

Cranberry Nut Snack Mix

When you're sitting around the living room after Thanksgiving dinner, this is a healthy and tasty snack to munch on.

Ingredients:

2 cups sunflower seeds
1 cup pine nuts
1 cup raw pumpkin seeds
1 cup dried and sweetened cranberries
1 cup raisins

Cooking utensil you'll need:
mixing bowl

Directions:

Pour all ingredients into mixing bowl and stir until well mixed. Transfer to a serving bowl. Makes 6 cups.

Thanksgiving Traditions

Food is a way of remembering. It connects us to our past, as families and as a nation. When we eat the same foods each Thanksgiving that we did the year before and the year before that, we create a long chain of memory that reaches back into the past. We taste the same flavors we have been putting in our mouths since we were very young children—and old memories are triggered, making us feel close to our parents and grandparents, and all those who have gone before us. As we taste the turkey and the pumpkin, the cranberries and the apples, the cinnamon and the molasses, we remember our history's deepest roots. We put tradition in our mouths and savor it, giving thanks for all we have been given.

Pulled Molasses Candy

Making this candy is as much fun as eating it. Colonial children often pulled the sticky candy as a party activity—and modern-day young people and adults find this a good treat to make on the evening of Thanksgiving Day.

Ingredients:

1 cup molasses
2 cups packed brown sugar
1 cup water
3 tablespoons cider vinegar
3 tablespoons butter or margarine

Cooking utensils you'll need:
measuring cups
measuring spoons
saucepan
baking sheet
paring knife
waxed paper

Directions:

Combine molasses, brown sugar, water, and vinegar in a saucepan, and cook over medium heat, stirring constantly, until mixture boils. Lower heat, and cook another 30 minutes, continuing to stir constantly, until mixture thickens. When ½ teaspoon dropped in a cup of cold water becomes brittle, the mixture is done. Add butter and stir; then pour onto a buttered baking sheet. When the mixture is cool enough to handle, butter your hands, and stretch and pull the candy until it is a light brown color. (This goes quicker and is more fun if several partners work on it together.) Cut in pieces and wrap in waxed paper.

Further Reading

Barth, Edna. *Turkeys, Pilgrims and Indian Corn: The Story of the Thanksgiving Symbols.* New York: Bt Bound, 2000.

Bleier, Edward. *The Thanksgiving Ceremony: New Traditions for America's Family Feast.* New York: Crown, 2003.

Morgan, Diane. *The Thanksgiving Table: Recipes and Ideas to Create Your Own Holiday Tradition.* New York: Chronicle, 2001.

Rainey, Barbara. *Thanksgiving: A Time to Remember.* New York: Crossway, 2002.

Rodgers, Rick. *Thanksgiving 101.* New York: Broadway, 1998.

Sanna, Ellyn. *Folk Festivals.* Philadelphia, Penn.: Mason Crest Publishers, 2003.

———. *Food Folklore.* Philadelphia, Penn.: Mason Crest Publishers, 2003.

Wilson, David Scofield and Angus Kress Gillespie. *Rooted in America: Folklore of Popular Fruits and Vegetables.* Knoxville: University of Tennessee Press, 1999.

Zanger, Mark H. *The American History Cookbook.* Westport, Conn.: Greenwood, 2003.

For More Information

American Indian Perspectives on Thanksgiving
www.2020tech.com/thanks/temp.html

The History of Thanksgiving
www.historychannel.com/exhibits/thanksgiving

Pilgrim History
www.pilgrimhall.org

Pumpkin History
www.urbanext.uiuc.edu/pumpkins/history.html

Thanksgiving Recipes
www.holidays.net/thanksgiving/recipes.htm

Publisher's note:
The Web sites listed on this page were active at the time of publication. The publisher is not responsible for Web sites that have changed their addresses or discontinued operation since the date of publication. The publisher will review and update the Web sites upon each reprint.

Index

Author:

Ellyn Sanna is the author of *101 Easy Supper Recipes for Busy Moms* from Promise Press, and several recipe gift books from Barbour Publishing, including *Feast, An Invitation to Tea*, and the books in the "Christmas at Home" series. A former middle school teacher and the mother of three children ages eleven through sixteen, she has experience addressing both the learning needs and the food tastes of young cooks. Ellyn Sanna has also authored and edited numerous educational titles.

Consultant:

The Culinary Institute of America is considered the world's premier culinary college. It is a private, not-for-profit learning institution, dedicated to providing the world's best culinary education. Its campuses in New York and California provide learning environments that focus on excellence, leadership, professionalism, ethics, and respect for diversity. The institute embodies a passion for food with first-class cooking expertise.

Recipe Contributor:

Patricia Therrien has worked for several years with Harding House Publishing Service as a researcher and recipe consultant—but she has been experimenting with food and recipes for the past thirty years. Her expertise has enriched the lives of friends and family. Patty lives in western New York State with her family and numerous animals, including several horses, cats, and dogs.

Picture Credits

Comstock: cover
Corel: pp. 9, 51, 68, 69
Photos.com: pp. 12, 15, 16, 18, 21, 22, 38, 39, 45, 52, 56, 72
PhotoDisc: cover, pp. 19, 20, 46, 49, 59, 69
BrandX: pp. 30, 42, 55
Corbis: pp. 50, 68
Benjamin Stewart: pp. 10, 23, 24, 27, 33, 37, 41, 60, 63, 64, 69